Polar Bear

Rod Theodorou

Heinemann Library
Chicago, Illinois

Designed by Ron Kamen
Illustrations by Dewi Morris/Robert Sydenham
Originated by Ambassador Litho Ltd.
Printed in Hong Kong/China

05 04 03 02 01
10 9 8 7 6 5 4 3 2 1

Library of Congress Cataloging-in-Publication Data
Theodorou, Rod.
    Polar bear / Rod Theodorou.
      p. cm. -- (Animals in danger)
    Includes bibliographical references and index (p.).
    ISBN 1-57572-273-9 (library)
    1. Polar bear--Juvenile literature. 2. Endangered species--Juvenile literature. [1. Polar bear. 2. Bears. 3. Endangered species.] I. Title.

QL737.C27 T478 2001
599.786--DC21   00-063260

Acknowledgments
The author and publishers are grateful to the following for permission to reproduce copyright material: B & C Alexander, p. 15; Ardea/Francois Gohier, p. 20; Ardea/Martin W. Grosnick, p. 4; Ardea/M. Watson, p. 26; Associated Press, p. 24; Bat Conservation International/Merlin D. Tuttle p. 4; BBC/Doug Allan, pp. 9, 14; BBC/Jeff Foott, pp. 5, 8, 25; BBC/Martha Holmes, p. 18; BBC/Thomas D. Mangelsen, pp. 16, 21; Bruce Coleman/Johnny Johnson, p. 6; Bruce Coleman/Dr. Scott Nielsen, p. 7; Bruce Coleman/John Shaw, p. 4; Bruce Coleman/Tom Schandy, p. 11; FLPA/F. Polking, p. 13; NHPA, p. 12; NHPA/Andy Rouse, p. 17; Oxford Scientific Films/Norbert Rosing, p. 27; Oxford Scientific Films/Skishoot-Offshoot, p. 23; Still Pictures/B & C Alexander, p. 22; WWF Photo Library/ Eric Dragesco, p. 19.

Cover photograph reproduced with permission of BBC Natural History Unit.

Every effort has been made to contact copyright holders of any material reproduced in this book. Any omissions will be rectified in subsequent printings if notice is given to the publisher.

Some words are shown in bold, **like this.** You can find out what they mean by looking in the glossary.

Contents

Animals in Danger

cheetah

koala

gray bat

All over the world, more than 25,000 animal **species** are in danger. Some are in danger because their homes are being destroyed. Many are in danger because people hunt them.

4

This book is about polar bears and why they are **endangered.** Unless people protect them, polar bears will become **extinct.** We will only be able to find out about them from books like this.

What Are Polar Bears?

Polar bears are **mammals**. They are the largest members of the bear family. They are also the largest **carnivores** in the world that live on land!

Polar bears are very good swimmers. They spend a lot of time in the ocean. They have thick fur and a layer of fat under their skin to keep them warm.

What Do Polar Bears Look Like?

Polar bears have a narrower head and longer nose than other bears. They also have smaller ears and are covered in white fur.

Polar bears have very large, wide paws that act like snowshoes. They have fur underneath their paws to keep them warm. The fur also keeps them from slipping on ice.

Where Do Polar Bears live?

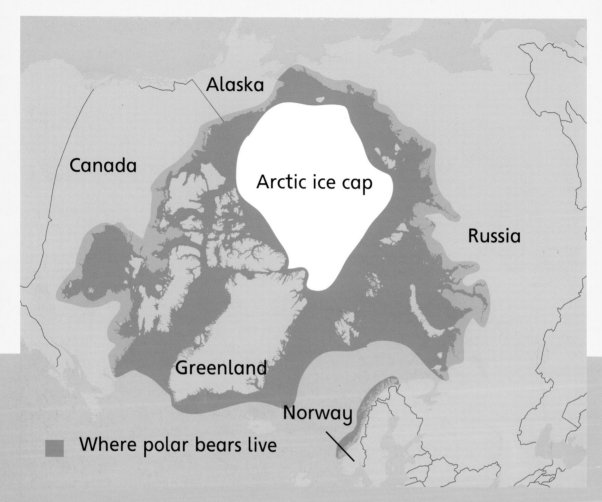

Alaska

Canada

Arctic ice cap

Russia

Greenland

Norway

■ Where polar bears live

Polar bears live on the frozen Arctic ice cap. They can also be found in Canada, Alaska, Greenland, northern Russia, and islands near Norway.

Polar bears like to live near the coast or out on the **sea ice.** There they can hunt their **prey.** They like to move around a lot, and they travel great distances every year.

What Do Polar Bears Eat?

Polar bears are **carnivores**. Their favorite **prey** is the ringed seal. A polar bear will dig into the ice or lie for hours near a **blow hole,** waiting to grab a seal with its sharp teeth and claws.

Polar bears will also attack young walruses. If
they are very hungry they will hunt smaller prey
such as sea birds and fish. Sometimes they even
eat plants or **forage** for trash.

Polar Bear Cubs

When a **female** polar bear is **pregnant** she digs a large **den** in the ice. Inside the den it is much warmer. Here she gives birth to one or two cubs.

The cubs are born around December. They are blind and about the size of a cat. The mother feeds them with her milk and they grow. Soon they are big enough to leave the den.

Caring for the Cubs

In March the **female** comes out of the **den**. The cubs are now the size of a medium-sized dog. They stay close to their mother as she leads them towards the coast to hunt.

16

The cubs watch how their mother hunts seals.
After two and a half years the mother leaves
her cubs. They are now big enough to hunt
for themselves.

Unusual Polar Bear Facts

Polar bear fur is so thick and warm that the bears can overheat! Sometimes they take a swim in freezing icy water just to cool down.

Male polar bears are much bigger than **females**. Sometimes the males have play fights. They both stand up and try to push each other over.

How Many Polar Bears Are There?

Thousands of years ago there were many more polar bears than there are today. In 1972 there were only about 8,500 polar bears left. The polar bear was close to becoming **extinct**.

The good news is that today there are about 24,000 polar bears alive. It is still very important that we help to **protect** bears for the future.

Why Is the Polar Bear in Danger?

Polar bears are so big and strong that they have no natural enemies. For thousands of years, humans have hunted polar bears for their thick, warm fur.

In the 1950s and 1960s, people started to hunt polar bears with snowmobiles and airplanes. The polar bears had nowhere to hide, and thousands were killed.

Oil **exploration** in the Arctic has harmed the polar bear. Oil spills poison the seals that the bears eat. Oil also ruins the polar bear's fur.

Polar bears need large areas of ice to live on. Some scientists think our whole planet is getting warmer. The polar ice may be melting. This is very bad for the bears. Pollution is also a **threat**.

How Is the Polar Bear Being Helped?

In 1973 the countries around the Arctic agreed to make the polar bear a **protected** species. They stopped most of the hunting. Now tourists hunt for polar bears—but only to take photographs!

Conservation groups such as the World Wildlife Foundation are working to stop illegal hunting and save the polar bear. They are also trying to teach people how harmful pollution is.

Polar Bear Fact File

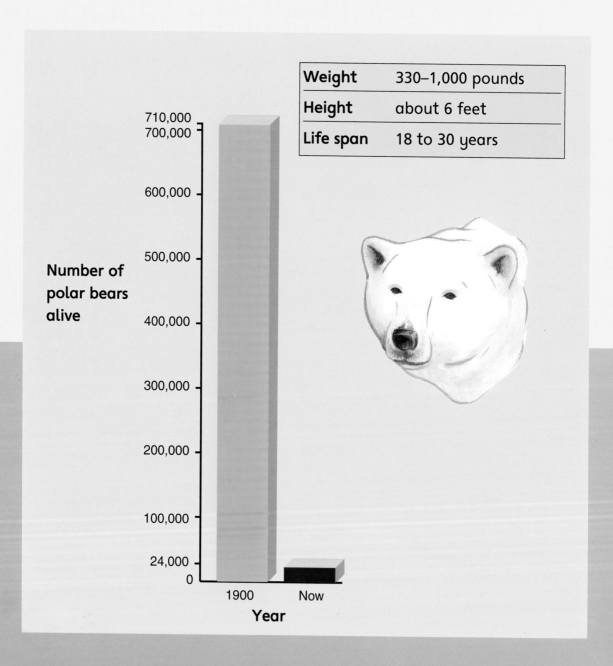

Weight	330–1,000 pounds
Height	about 6 feet
Life span	18 to 30 years

Number of polar bears alive

710,000
700,000

600,000

500,000

400,000

300,000

200,000

100,000

24,000
0

1900   Now

Year

World Danger Table

	Number when animal was listed as endangered	Number that may be alive today
Polar bear	8,500	24,000
Black bear	The black bear is not **endangered**.	18,000
Grizzly bear	50,000	800–1,000
Sloth bear	7,000–8,000	about 10,000
Spectacled bear	The spectacled bear is not endangered.	10,000

There are many other bears in the world that are in danger of becoming **extinct**. This table shows some of these animals.

How Can You Help the Polar Bear?

If you and your friends raise money for the polar bear, you can send it to these organizations. They take the money and use it to pay **conservation** workers and to buy food and tools to help save the polar bear.

Defenders of Wildlife
1101 Fourteenth St., N.W. #1400
Washington, DC 20005

World Wildlife Fund
1250 Twenty-fourth St.
P.O. Box 97180
Washington, DC 20037

More Books to Read

Hodge, Deborah. *Bears: Polar Bears, Black Bears, and Grizzly Bears.* Buffalo, N.Y.: Kids Can Press, 1999.

Patent, Dorothy. *Great Ice Bear: The Polar Bear and the Eskimo.* New York: Morrow Avon, 1999.

Robinson, Claire. *Bears.* Chicago: Heinemann Library, 1999.

Glossary

blow hole	hole in the ice where seals come up to breathe air
carnivore	animal that eats only meat
conservation	looking after things, especially if they are in danger
den	safe place where animals can sleep or rest
endangered	group of animals that is dying out, so there are few left
exploration	visiting a place to find out what is there
extinct	group of animals that has died out and can never live again
female	girl or woman
forage	to try to find food
male	boy or man
mammal	animal with hair, like a human or a dog, that drinks its mother's milk as a baby
pregnant	when a female animal is going to have a baby
prey	animals that are hunted and killed by other animals
protect	to keep safe
sea ice	ice that floats on the sea
species	group of animals or plants that are very similar
threat	something that puts an animal in danger

31

Index